Easy Lessons

for

Teaching

Word Families

by Judy Lynch

NEW YORK • TORONTO • LONDON • AUCKLAND • SYDNEY
MEXICO CITY • NEW DELHI • HONG KONG

Dedication:

To my coach Mike and our team:
Kevin, Shannon & Michael

Acknowledgments:

Grateful thanks to my mentors:
Bev Ruby and Linda Lake, Reading Recovery® Teacher Leaders
Cecil Morris, California Reading and Literature Project
Dr. Mary Barr, Center for Language and Learning
Dr. Richard Herzberg, Bureau of Education and Research

Heartfelt gratitude to Pat Cunningham and Dottie Hall, authors of *Making Words,*
for their inspiration and support of classroom teachers.

And to the first-grade teachers at Madison Elementary, Sacramento, who field tested these
lessons: Jordy Banner, Mary Ann Blohm-Craig, Cecelia Kingsbury, Heather Smith, and
Sherry Valiska

Cover design by Jaime Lucero
Cover illustration by Amanda Haley
Interior design by LDL Designs
Interior illustrations by Maxie Chambliss

ISBN 0-590-68570-8

Copyright © 1998 by Judy Lynch

Table of Contents

Introduction

❖ What Is *Easy Lessons* ❖ for Teaching Word Families?

Easy Lessons is a practical guide for teachers that links phonemic awareness (hearing sounds in words) with phonics (the visual details of print).

The first steps into making this important link need to be made with modeling and coaching. This hands-on activity provides systematic lessons that improve spelling, reading, phonemic awareness and phonics. In about a 20-minute lesson, students manipulate their own letters to make words having high frequency word patterns. The group later sorts these for common patterns and reads and writes more words using the sounds they have just practiced. The link to word patterns is further reinforced in the context of nursery rhymes. This book is designed to be "user-friendly" for teachers so it has simple lesson plans and all the materials ready to make.

❖ Why a new book? ❖

Pat Cunningham and Dottie Hall have changed phonics instruction in classrooms across the United States with their book *Making Words* (Good Apple, 1994). I have been one of their cheerleaders as I've demonstrated to teachers these hands-on, research based phonics lessons. Then why would I presume to write a book that is similar but has important differences?

I wrote *Easy Lessons for Teaching Word Families* because I was concerned that *Making Words* was too challenging for some of our first graders. Before *Making Words,* they needed simpler lessons closer to the "Making and Breaking" component of the Reading Recovery® lesson. As a Reading Recovery® teacher working with the most at-risk first graders, I do these basic lessons daily that link phonemic awareness to print while teaching word patterns. Pat Cunningham was inspired by these Reading Recovery® lessons when she developed her word lessons (*Reading Teacher,* September, 1992). I have since discovered that first graders in *regular* classrooms profit from *Easy Lessons* as they solidify the link between sounds they hear (phonemic awareness) and which letters make those sounds (phonics). At the kindergarten level, I have used *Easy Lessons* with small groups of students who know their letters in isolation but don't know what to do with them in words. ESL and Title 1 students also benefit from teacher coaching during these simplified lessons using letters as manipulatives.

❖ Key Points ❖

Easy Lessons for Teaching Word Families is designed for small groups of students who know 20 or more lowercase letters. Built in practice with a letter/sound in a lesson and across lessons will help teach unknown letters. Lessons are grouped by vowel patterns to help teachers pick and choose lessons needed by their students.

The Wordboards provide boxes that represent each sound heard in a word. These boxes make a 1:1 match for students linking sound to print. Putting sounds in boxes is based on the work of Elkonin and is very effective in Reading Recovery® and in classroom practice.

I wrote *Easy Lessons for Teaching Word Families* also to emphasize the highest utility spelling patterns. Durrell's research found that the 37 most common phonograms make up 500 primary words. The decoding of this unit of print is more reliable than following old rules we used to teach. "Two vowels go walking, the first one does the talking" is only true in less than 50 percent of words. Pat Cunningham (1991) reminds us that the brain is a pattern detector, not a rule applier. There are many word patterns we can teach, but I wanted to build lessons based specifically on those with the highest use for emergent readers and writers. The research on onset and rime (vowel patterns in syllables) has explained why teachers have always had success with what we used to call "word families," ie. *cat, sat, chat*. Treiman (1985) found that the break of words into vowel patterns by syllables is a "psychological reality." Research into decoding by analogy (Goswami and Bryant, 1990) shows that students can use a known word

(cat) to read and spell unknown words *(splat)*.

Before giving students individual letters to manipulate, I model the process and use only the large letters in the pocket chart. This gives me an opportunity to talk them through the process of listening for sounds and pinpointing where they hear the changes as we make a new scrambled word. The new research on phonemic awareness points out how crucial it is for students to hear individual sounds in the speech stream. When they become flexible with that, I add letters to make the essential link to phonics.

Terminology Talk

Teacher		How to describe these terms to kids

Onset

- Consonants up to a vowel in a syllable *(shot)*   ⟷   • Letters up to a vowel in a word

Rime

- Vowel pattern in a syllable *(shot)*
- Spelling Pattern   ⟷   • Chunk
  - Looks the same. Sounds the same

Rhyme

- Words that sound the same but may have a different spelling pattern: *got, taught, fought*   ⟷   • Words that sound the same but may look different at the end

Nonsense Words

- Nonsense words that may come up when children brainstorm rimes or rhymes: not, pot, **zot**   ⟷   • Words that Dr. Seuss might use in a book he wrote.

Phonemic Awareness

- Hearing discreet sounds in the speech stream.
- Hearing spoken words, syllables, sounds (phonemes)   ⟷   • "Use your ears..."
  - "Listen..."

Phonics

- Sound/Symbol Correspondence
- Letters and patterns of print
- Visual   ⟷   • "Use your eyes ..."
  - "Does that look right?"
  - "Look"

Easy Lessons for Teaching Word Families • Scholastic Professional Books

Basic Materials

Nursery Rhymes (Appendix A)

Link the common patterns practiced in *Easy Lessons* to favorite nursery rhymes that can be put in your pocket chart. Black line masters for individual student copies are available.

Large Letter Cards (Appendix B)

Photocopy, laminate, and use in the pocket chart.

Small Letter Cards (Appendix C) or Magnetic Letters

Photocopy for the students to manipulate to make the words.

Letter Boxes/Word Boards (Appendix D)

Boxes are made to match 3- to 5-letter words. This encourages students to match the sounds they hear to the correct boxes going left to right.

or

Magnetic Boards

Individual magnetic boards can be found in the housewares department of Target, Walmart, K-Mart, etc. They are sold as burner covers.

Pocket Chart

Teacher and students can manipulate large letters here to make words. They can add word cards as they make and sort new words.

Small Word Cards

Use 3-by-5-inch index cards to write each word featured in the lesson.

1, 2, Buckle My Shoe

1, 2,   Buckle my shoe

3, 4,   Shut the door

5, 6,   Pick up sticks

7, 8   Lay them straight

9, 10   The big fat hen

High Utility Patterns/Rimes
For Spelling Patterns and Rhymes

cat   **bat**   **cake**   **snake**

Wylie and Durrell (1970) identified 37 phonograms which could be found in almost 500 primary grade words:

ack	ail	ain	ake	ale
ame	an	ank	ap	ash
at	ate	aw	ay	eat
ell	est	ice	ick	ide
ight	ill	in	ine	ing
ink	ip	it	ock	oke
op	ore	ot	uck	ug
ump	unk			

Easy Lessons for Teaching Word Families • Scholastic Professional Books

Lesson	Featured Patterns	Lesson	Featured Patterns
1	an, ap	29	ack, ame
2	ash, at	30	ake, at, ate
3	at	31	ame, an, ap
4	op, ot	32	ale, ake
5	ock, ot	33	oke, op
6	ock	34	ock, oke
7	it	35	ore, oke
8	ip, it	36	ice, ide
9	in, ing	37	ide, in, ine
10	ing	38	ill, in, ine
11	ink	39	ice, ick, in, ine
12	in, ing, ink	40	ap, at, aw
13	uck, ug	41	aw, ay
14	ump	42	an, ap, aw
15	uck, ump, unk	43	an, ash, ay
16	ell	44	op, ot
17	ell	45	ight, it
18	est	46	ight, ing, ink
19	an, ap, in, ip	47	in, ight, it
20	at, it	48	an, ank, unk
21	ack, at, ick	49	ail, ain, in, ip
22	ash	50	ame, ore
23	an, at, est	51	ail, ain, ip, op
24	ug	52	ail, ap, ill, ip
25	op, ot	53	ate, eat
26	ell, ill, it	54	ug, ate
27	est, ock, ot	55	ain, an, ank, in, ink
28	ale, an, ank, ap		

Pattern	Lessons That Feature the Pattern	Pattern	Lessons That Feature the Pattern
ack	21, 29	ight	45, 46, 47
ail	49, 51, 52	ill	38, 52
ain	49, 51, 55	in	9, 12, 19, 37, 41, 47, 49, 55
ake	30, 32		
ale	28, 32	ine	37, 38, 39
ame	29, 31, 50	ing	9, 10, 12, 46
an	1, 19, 23, 28, 31, 42, 43, 48, 49, 55	ink	11, 12, 46, 55
ank	28, 48, 55	ip	19, 49, 51, 52
ap	1, 19, 28, 31, 40, 42, 51, 52	it	7, 8, 20, 26, 45, 47
ash	2, 43	ock	5, 6, 34, 54
at	2, 20, 21, 23, 27, 30, 40	oke	33, 34, 35
		op	4, 25, 33, 44
ate	30, 53, 54	ore	35, 50
aw	40, 41, 42	ot	4, 5, 25, 27, 44
ay	41, 43	uck	13, 15
eat	53	ug	13, 24, 54
ell	16, 17, 26	ump	14, 15
est	18, 23	unk	15, 48
ice	36, 39		
ick	21, 39		
ide	36, 37		

Easy Lessons for Teaching Word Families • Scholastic Professional Books

Lesson Format: A Sample Lesson

To help you understand how to guide each of the lessons in this book, here is how I would conduct Lesson #1.

STEP 1: Collect Lesson Materials

Before the lesson, I gather materials. For Lesson #1, I will be working with the letters *a, c, m, n, p, r, t*. I pull out my large letter cards (see Appendix B) for the pocket chart and the small paper letters my students will use (see Appendix C). If I have children who I think will benefit from using even more concrete manipulatives than the letter cards, I'll pull out the magnetic letters and trays. This prep takes just a few minutes.

STEPS 2 & 3: Make and Coach

With four to ten students ready to start, we pass the word boards around the table from left to right. Then we pass and place the letters on the bottom of each board quickly—I stress that we do not play with letters.

❖ Tips for Storing the Materials

I store the small letter cards in clear plastic drawers, which you can buy inexpensively in discount stores and hardware stores; they're often sold near tool boxes. I label each drawer with a letter. The word boards are in file folders beside the shelf; the 3-by-5-inch word cards are kept in envelopes marked with the lesson number, stored in a plastic box. I keep magnetic letters and magnetic trays in nearby box. The magnetic trays are actually burner covers, which you can buy in houseware stores.

I dictate each word, tell how many letters to use, and use it in a sentence or explain its meaning to provide a context for each word. Here is a typical dialogue from Lesson 1:

Teacher: Today we are going to make a lot of words with our letters. We'll need to use our ears to listen for sounds and we'll need our eyes to look for the letters to match those sounds. Let's make sure you know the letter names and sounds.

What is it? (I point to the first letter, *a*.) *What sound does it make? /a/* (I continue to quickly name letters and sounds).

Ready? Let's make some words.

Number 1, cap. *The baseball player wears a cap on his head. Cap. Say it slowly:* c-a-p. *What do you hear first? Put that letter in the first box. Say it again:* c-a-p... *What do you hear in the middle? Say it again and run your finger under the letters. What do you hear at the end? Check it with your finger—does it look right?*

(As students finish, I call one student up to make the word with the large letter cards in the pocket chart. Everyone checks his or her answer by looking at the pocket chart.)

*Run your finger under the word and pull the sounds across to blend them into a word—*c-a-p. (Students make this motion, and blend the word out loud). *Good! When we read words we don't say, /c/ /c/ /c/-/a/ /a/ /a/-/p/ /p/ /p/. That doesn't sound like a word, does it?*

#2. Now you will change one letter. Look at your word and see which one should be changed before you move any letters.

Map. *We used a map to find our way in the car.* Map. *Run your finger under the word— where do you hear the change?*

(I continue to coach individuals or the group as needed with advice, such as:

Say it slowly. What do you hear? Where do you hear it? What letter makes that sound?

Now run your finger under and read. (I invite a student volunteer to make the word in the pocket chart, using the large letters. I place the 3-by-5-inch word card beneath the first word, *cap*. Now we are ready to move on to the next word.)

#3. Change one letter—look to see whether the change is in the beginning, the middle, or the end. Tap. Water from the faucet is called tap water. Tap.

(I coach, then invite a student to make the word in the pocket chart.)

 # 4. Change one letter—listen for where you hear the change. Rap. Teenagers like rap music. Rap.

#5. Change one letter—be ready! Nap. The baby took a nap after lunch. Nap.

cap
tap
rap
nap
pan
ran
tan
can
man

#6. Now, use the same letters to make a new word. Be careful; listen to each sound and then look for the letter to match. Pan. The dinner was cooked in the pan. Pan.

#7. Change one letter to make a new word. Ran. The girl ran at recess. Ran

#8. Change one letter: Tan. The color tan is light brown. Tan

#9. Change one letter. Can. Can you come to my house? Can.

#10. Change one letter. Man. The man delivered a pizza to our house. Man.
(Most lessons include one or two challenge words to use when you feel children are ready for more complex words.)

STEP 4: Sort

Teacher: It's time to put our letters away. (Collect the letters and the word boards. Now the focus will be on sorting the 3-by-5-inch word cards in the pocket chart by rime patterns/word families). *Let's look at the words we have made in our pocket chart. Today we are going to find words that have the same chunk—the groups of letters at the end of a word that look the same and sound the same.*

Here's the word tap *and the word* map. *Say them. What chunk is the same at the end of each word?* ("Ap," the students respond.)

Good. Who can find another word with the same chunk at the end? (Children proceed to find the other *ap* words. Each time we put another word in our group, we say the words to make sure they sound the same at the end. We look carefully for the same chunk at the end. We have just practiced phonemic awareness and phonics.)

Do rap *and* tan *have the same chunk at the end? Does it look the same and sound the same? Let's look. Let's say them and see. Is there a word with the same chunk as* tan? (We make another column of *an* words and look at the end of each and listen for the same sound.)

Today we have been helping our brain to figure out words it doesn't know. If we read a word we don't know, our brain looks for a chunk at the end that it knows. So if we can read map, *then our brain looks at* cap *and sees a part it knows—*ap. *This makes it easier for us to say, Yes! I got it!* Cap.

STEP 5: Find

Teacher: Boys and girls, it's time to look carefully at two letters that sometimes trick kids because they look alike. But let's have sharp eyes to see how they are different. (I show an *n* to the group.)

Tell me what this looks like. (I accept all answers that describe the shape, size, direction, or unique features.)

Marta: It looks like a stool to put my feet on, all round on top with legs.
Ryan: To me, it looks like a worm with one bump.
Karly: I see a line with one hump in front.
Teacher: Good. You are looking carefully and it reminds you of some things you know. It has a short line and one bump in front. This is an n. *Is this an* n? (I show an *m.)*
Ryan: No, that is a worm with two bumps.
Akeem: No, look, there are too many bumps.
Teacher: Wow! I thought I could trick you, but you are looking too carefully for me to get you today. Let's look at the word cards and see how many m's *we can find.* (As students locate letters, I continue to question what makes that an *m.* Then we quickly find some *n's* and continue to mention their unique physical characteristics.)

STEP 6: Can You Write?

Each lesson usually ends with reading and writing words with the same word family. I have scratch paper or white boards handy for students to write a few words using the rime patterns/word families that we practiced in the lesson today. They have to make links between the known and the unknown, and use the patterns to build skills that transfer to spelling.

Teacher: Now let's write some words that are like the words we made today. I can't teach you every word in the English language, but I can show you how to use words you know to write words that are new to you. Listen carefully and think about what chunk you hear at the end of the words I say and then write the letters to match.
Fan. It was so hot I had to fan myself. Fan. *Say it very slowly and then listen for the first sound—that's it. Now say it again. Let's check by running our finger under the word. Does it look right?*
(Repeat process with the word *lap,* coaching and checking as students write.)

STEP 7: Can You Read?

I grab my small white board and write a couple new words for students to read/decode. In doing this, I am making sure that students know they can apply what they've learned in this lesson when they read independently. When they come to a word they have never seen before, they can figure it out by using the chunks they know.

Teacher: Now it's my turn to write some words with the chunks you have learned. I want to see how well you can read new words. Don't shout out your answer, just say the word softly—look for the part you know!

I write *van. We drove this on our trip.*
I make sure they have all blended the sounds and then we respond together.

Teacher: What is the chunk in van?
(*An,* students say.)
That's right! We made the word pan *in our lesson and now you can read brand new words with that chunk. When your brain sees something it knows in a word that is new, the part you know will pop right out to help you read it.*

I repeat step 7 with the word *sap.*

PRACTICE

I use the practice time to link the lesson to a nursery rhyme or other poem we have. (The poems are either in poem boards or on pocket chart strips that we use for shared reading.)

Teacher: I have a poem today that has our chunk an *in it. Let's read "Georgy Porgy" together.* (See Appendix A for nursery rhymes and suggestions for working with them.)

Lesson 1

Letters: a c m n p r t

Make:

cap

map

tap

rap

nap/

pan

ran

tan

can

man

Sort:

ap   an   rimes

Find:

m's and n's

Can you write?:

(Students write words with same patterns)

fan   lap

Can you read?:

(Teacher writes the word for them to read)

van   sap

Practice:

Practice the common pattern *an* in "Simple Simon," "Georgy Porgy," and others in Appendix A.

Easy Lessons for Teaching Word Families • Scholastic Professional Books

Letters: a b c h m s t

Make:

sat

mat

cat

hat

bat

bash

cash

mash

rash

rat

chat
(CHALLENGE)

Sort:

at   ash   rimes

Find:

c's and a's

Can you write?:

(Students write words with same patterns)

vat   lash

Can you read?:

(Teacher writes the word for them to read)

brat   dash

Practice:

Practice the common pattern *at* in "Pat-a-Cake," "The Ten O'Clock Scholar," and "1, 2, Buckle My Shoe" in Appendix A.

Lesson 3
Letters: a b c f h m p s t

Make:

at

cat

cab

pat

sat

fat

hat

has

ham

bam

bat

cabs
(CHALLENGE)

cats
(CHALLENGE)

Sort:

at   am   rimes

Find:

p's and b's

Can you write?:

(Students write words with same patterns)

ram   rat

Can you read?:

(Teacher writes the word for them to read)

splat   ram

Practice:

Practice the common pattern *at* in "Little Miss Muffet," "Jack Sprat," and others in Appendix A.

Easy Lessons for Teaching Word Families • Scholastic Professional Books

Letters: o b c g h l p r t

Make:

hop

cop

lop

top/

pot

rot

hot

cot

lot

lob

rob

gob

got

chop
(CHALLENGE)

Sort:

op   ot   ob   rimes

Find:

l's and t's

Can you write?:

(Students write words with same patterns)

job   stop

Can you read?:

(Teacher writes the word for them to read)

pop   spot

Practice:

Practice the common pattern *ot* in "Pease Porridge Hot" and "Little Boy Blue" in Appendix A.

Lesson 5
Letters: o c d k l p r t

Make:

lot

lock

rock

rot

dot

dock

cod

rod

pod

pot

pock

plot

(CHALLENGE)

Sort:

ot   ock   od   rimes

Find:

d's and p's

Can you write?:

(Students write words with same patterns)

nod   clock

Can you read?:

(Teacher writes the word for them to read)

slot   sock

Practice:

Practice the common pattern *ock* in "Hickory Dickory Dock," "Birds of a Feather," and "Sing a Song" in Appendix A.

Letters: o c f h l k r s t

Make:

rock

sock

lock

lost

cost

frost

frock

tock

hock

shock
(CHALLENGE)

clock
(CHALLENGE)

Sort:

ock   ost   rimes

Find:

c's and o's

Can you write?:

(Students write words with same patterns)

dock   block

Can you read?:

(Teacher writes the word for them to read)

crock   flock

Practice:

Practice the common pattern *ock* in "Rock a Bye Baby," "Sing a Song," and "Ten O'Clock Scholar in Appendix A.

Letters: i d f h k l m s t

Make:

it

sit

kit

fit

lit

hit

him

his

hid

kid

lid

skid
(CHALLENGE)

skit
(CHALLENGE)

Sort:

it   id   rimes

Find:

h's and d's

Can you write?:

(Students write words with same patterns)

bit   Sid

Can you read?:

(Teacher writes the word for them to read)

pit   grid

Practice:

Practice the common pattern *it* in "Pat-a-Cake," "The Clever Hen," and "Cross Patch" in Appendix A.

Letters: i h l p r s t

Make:

rip

lip

hip

sip

tip/

pit

sit

hit

lit

it

trip
(CHALLENGE)

ship
(CHALLENGE)

Sort:

ip   it   rimes

Find:

l's and i's

Can you write?:

(Students write words with same patterns)

fit   dip

Can you read?:

(Teacher writes the word for them to read)

flip   skit

Practice:

Practice the common pattern *ip* in "Billy, Billy" and "I Saw a Ship A-Sailing" in Appendix A.

Letters: i b d g n r s t w

Make:

in

tin

bin

din

win

wing

sing

ring

swing
(CHALLENGE)

string
(CHALLENGE)

bring
(CHALLENGE)

Sort:

in   ing   rimes

Find:

n's and w's

Can you write?:

(Students write words with same patterns)

fin   bing

Can you read?:

(Teacher writes the word for them to read)

chin   king

Practice:

Practice the common patterns *in* and *ing* in "Sing a Song" and "Ding Dong Bell" in Appendix A.

Lesson 10

Letters: i b g n p r s t w

Make:

ring

bing

bring

wing

sing

swing

sting

ping

spring

brings
(CHALLENGE)

Sort:

ing   rimes
(4 & 5 letter words)

Find:

p's and g's

Can you write?:

(Students write words with same patterns)

king   thing

Can you read?:

(Teacher writes the word for them to read)

ding   sling

Practice:

Practice the common pattern *ing* in "Banbury Cross," "Jack and Jill," and "Old Mother Hubbard" in Appendix A.

Scholastic Professional Books • *Easy Lessons for Teaching Word Families*   ✤23

Letters: i b d k l n r s t

Make:

ink

link

blink

brink

rink

drink

sink

slink

stink

drinks
(CHALLENGE)

Sort:

ink   rimes
(three- & four-letter words)

Find:

b's and k's

Can you write?:

(Students write words with same patterns)

pink   kink

Can you read?:

(Teacher writes the word for them to read)

wink   think

Practice:

Practice the common pattern *ink* in "Twinkle Twinkle Little Star" and "Cross Patch" in Appendix A.

Letters: i g k n p r s w

Make:

pin

win

kin

king

ring

rink

pink

sink

sing

ping

wing

wink

wings

(CHALLENGE)

Sort:

in   ing   ink   rimes

Find:

r's and n's

Can you write?:

(Students write words with same patterns)

tin   sting

Can you read?:

(Teacher writes the word for them to read)

spin   stink

Practice:

Practice the common pattern *ing* in "Ding Dong Bell," "Humpty Dumpty," and "The Hobby Horse" in Appendix A.

Lesson 13
Letters: u b c g h k r s t

Make:

bus

bug

hug

hut

rut

rug

tug

tuck

buck

suck

chug

(CHALLENGE)

Sort:

ug   uck   rimes

Find:

b's and h's

Can you write?:

(Students write words with same patterns)

jug   duck

Can you read?:

(Teacher writes the word for them to read)

plug   luck

Practice:

Practice the common pattern *uck* in "One, Two, Buckle My Shoe" and "Hickory Dickory Dock" in Appendix A.

Easy Lessons for Teaching Word Families • Scholastic Professional Books

Letters: u b d h j m p r

Make:

mud

bud

bum

bump

jump

dump

rump

hump

lump/

plum

rum

hum

drum
(CHALLENGE)

Sort:

ump   um   rimes

Find:

u's and m's

Can you write?:

(Students write words with same patterns)

stump   yum

Can you read?:

(Teacher writes the word for them to read)

sum   grump

Practice:

Practice the common pattern *ump* in "Humpty Dumpty" and "The Pumpkin Eater" in Appendix A.

Letters: u b c d k l n s

Make:

sunk

dunk

bunk

buck

suck

duck

dump

bump

lump

luck

bumps
(CHALLENGE)

Sort:

unk   uck   ump   rimes

Find:

m's and n's

Can you write?:

(Students write words with same patterns)

yuck   junk

Can you read?:

(Teacher writes the word for them to read)

skunk   truck

Practice:

Practice the common pattern *ump* in "The Cat and the Fiddle" and "Humpty Dumpty" in Appendix A.

Lesson 16

Letters: e b j l l s t w y

Make:

bet

bell

sell

set

jet

jell

well

wet

yet

yell

yells
(CHALLENGE)

Sort:

ell   et   rimes

Find:

j's and y's

Can you write?:

(Students write words with same patterns)

tell   spell

Can you read?:

(Teacher writes the word for them to read)

net   Nell

Practice:

Practice the common pattern *ell* in "Cock-Crow," "Jack and Jill," "Banbury Cross," and "The Pumpkin Eater" in Appendix A.

Letters: e b f h l l m s t

Make:

bet

set

met

melt

belt

felt

fell

bell

tell

sell

smell
(CHALLENGE)

shell
(CHALLENGE)

Sort:

ell   elt   rimes

Find:

f's and t's

Can you write?:

(Students write words with same patterns)

jell   pelt

Can you read?:

(Teacher writes the word for them to read)

welt   yell

Practice:

Practice the common pattern *ell* in "The Pumpkin Eater," "Little Bo Peep," and "Jack and Jill" in Appendix A.

Easy Lessons for Teaching Word Families • Scholastic Professional Books

Letters: e b n p s t t

Make:

pet

set

bet

net/

ten

tent

bent

best

nest

test

pest

step
(CHALLENGE)

spent
(CHALLENGE)

Sort:

est   et   ent   rimes

Find:

b's and p's

Can you write?:

(Students write words with same patterns)

went   rest

Can you read?:

(Teacher writes the word for them to read)

vest   wet

Practice:

Practice the common pattern *est*

in "Thirty Days Hath September"

in Appendix A.

Letters: a i f n p r s

Make:

sap

nap/

pan

pin/

nip

rip

rap

ran

fan

fin

snap
(CHALLENGE)

pins
(CHALLENGE)

Sort:

ap   an   ip   in   rimes

Find:

r's and n's

Can you write?:

(Students write words with same patterns)

slap   flip

Can you read?:

(Teacher writes the word for them to read)

bran   chin

Practice:

Practice the common patterns *an* and *ip* in "I Saw a Ship A-Sailing" or *ip* in "Billy Billy" in Appendix A.

Lesson 20

Letters: a i b c f h p s t

Make:

at

cat

fat

bat

bit

fit

sit

hit

pit

pat

cast
(CHALLENGE)

spit
(CHALLENGE)

Sort:

at   it   rimes

Find:

h's and b's

Can you write?:

(Students write words with same patterns)

that   omit

Can you read?:

(Teacher writes the word for them to read)

split   splat

Practice:

Practice the common patterns *at* and *it* in "Little Miss Muffet," "Hey Diddle Diddle," and "Ding Dong Bell" in Appendix A.

Lesson 21
Letters: a i b c k r s t

Make:

at

rat

cat

bat

back

rack

tack

track

sack

stack

stick

sick

tick

trick

(CHALLENGE)

brick

(CHALLENGE)

Sort:

at   ack   ick   rimes

Find:

c's and a's

Can you write?:

(Students write words with same patterns)

pack   chick

Can you read?:

(Teacher writes the word for them to read)

quick   quack

Practice:

Practice the common patterns *at*, *ick*, and *ack* in "Jack Sprat" in Appendix A.

Easy Lessons for Teaching Word Families • Scholastic Professional Books

Lesson 22

Letters: a i c d f h r s w

Make:

as

has/

ash

cash

crash

rash

dash

dish

fish

wish

Sort:

ash   ish   as   rimes

Find:

d's and h's

Can you write?:

(Students write words with same patterns)

swish   smash

Can you read?:

(Teacher writes the word for them to read)

squish   flash

Practice:

Practice the common pattern *ash* in "Dapple Gray" and "If All the Seas" in Appendix A.

Letters: a e b c n p r s t

Make:

cat

can

pan

pen

pet

pat

bat

bet

best

rest

pest

past

cast

crest
(CHALLENGE)

Sort:

at   an   est   rimes

Find:

a's and e's

Can you write?:

(Students write words with same patterns)

nest   jet

Can you read?:

(Teacher writes the word for them to read)

blast   chest

Practice:

Practice the common patterns *at* and *an* in "Pat-a-Cake," "The Cat and the Fiddle," and "If All the Seas" in Appendix A.

Letters: o u c g h n p r t

Make:

cut

hut

hot

rot

pot

pug

hug

tug/

gut

gun

rut

rug

chug

(CHALLENGE)

Sort:

ug   ot   ut   rimes

Find:

p's and g's

Can you write?:

(Students write words with same patterns)

slug   slot

Can you read?:

(Teacher writes the word for them to read)

trot   drug

Practice:

Practice the common pattern *ot* in "Pease Porridge," "Simple Simon," and "Old Mother Hubbard" in Appendix A.

Letters: o u b c h m p r t

Make:

mob

mop

hop

cop

cup

cub

rub

rob

rot

hot

pot/

top

chop

(CHALLENGE)

Sort:

op   ot   rimes

Find:

c's and o's

Can you write?:

(Students write words with same patterns)

shop   shot

Can you read?:

(Teacher writes the word for them to read)

drop   gumdrop

Practice:

Practice the common pattern *op* in

"Rock-a-Bye Baby" in Appendix A.

Easy Lessons for Teaching Word Families • Scholastic Professional Books

Letters: e i b l l m p s t

Make:

it
lit
bit
pit
pill
mill
sill
sell
tell
till
bill
bell
spill
(CHALLENGE)
smell
(CHALLENGE)

Sort:

ell   ill   it   rimes

Find:

l's and t's

Can you write?:

(Students write words with same patterns)

jell   hill

Can you read?:

(Teacher writes the word for them to read)

chill   yell

Practice:

Practice the common pattern *ill* in "The Ten O'Clock Scholar," "Little Boy Blue," and "The Clever Hen" in Appendix A.

Letters: o e c d k p r s t

Make:

sod

pod

pot

rot

cot

dot

dock

sock

rock

rod

red

rest

pest

crest

(CHALLENGE)

stock

(CHALLENGE)

Sort:

est   ock   ot   rimes

Find:

p's and d's

Can you write?:

(Students write words with same patterns)

jest   clock

Can you read?:

(Teacher writes the word for them to read)

shock   vest

Practice:

Practice the common pattern *ock* in "Sing a Song of Sixpence," "Rock-a-Bye Baby," and "Hickory Dickory Dock" in Appendix A.

Lesson 28

Letters: a e b k l n p s t

Make:

an

pan/

nap

nab/

ban

bank

sank

tank

lank

lap/

pal

pale

tale

sale

stale
(CHALLENGE)

Sort:

ale   an   ank   rimes

Find:

p's and b's

Can you write?:

(Students write words with same patterns)

gale   van

Can you read?:

(Teacher writes the word for them to read)

ran   thank

Practice:

Practice the common pattern *ale* in "Simple Simon" and "The Clever Hen" in Appendix A.

Letters: a e b c k l m s t

Make:

came

same

tame

lame

blame

black

back

sack

stack

tack

lack

backs

(CHALLENGE)

tacks

(CHALLENGE)

Sort:

ack   ame   rimes

Find:

l's and b's

Can you write?:

(Students write words with same patterns)

game   black

Can you read?:

(Teacher writes the word for them to read)

snack   frame

Practice:

Practice the common patterns *ack* and *ame* in "Jack and Jill" in Appendix A.

Lesson 30

Letters: a e b c h k l s t

Make:

at

bat

cat

sat

hat

hate

late

lake

bake

cake

take

sake

shake
(CHALLENGE)

stake
(CHALLENGE)

Sort:

at   ate   ake   rimes

Find:

h's and b's

Can you write?:

(Students write words with same patterns)

date   bake

Can you read?:

(Teacher writes the word for them to read)

snake   plate

Practice:

Practice the common patterns *ake* and *ate* in "The Greedy Man" or *ate* in "Cock-Crow" in Appendix A.

Letters: a e c m n p s t

Make:

an

tan

pan/

nap

cap

tap

sap

sam

same

tame

name

came

Stan
(CHALLENGE)

maps
(CHALLENGE)

Sort:

an   ap   ame   rimes

Find:

n's and m's

Can you write?:

(Students write words with same patterns)

fame   plan

Can you read?:

(Teacher writes the word for them to read)

than   frame

Practice:

Practice the common patterns *an* and *ap* in "The Hobby Horse" and "Sing a Song" in Appendix A.

Letters: a e b k l m s t

Make:

ale

sale

tale

stale

stake

sake

take

bake

bale

lake

make

male

bakes
(CHALLENGE)

Sort:

ake   ale   rimes

Find:

k's and b's

Can you write?:

(Students write words with same patterns)

scale   flake

Can you read?:

(Teacher writes the word for them to read)

wake   whale

Practice:

Practice the common patterns *ake* and *ale* in "The Clever Hen" in Appendix A.

Letters: e o c h k m p r s

Make:

mop

hop

cop

crop

chop

poke

coke

choke

smoke

spoke

chops
(CHALLENGE)

Sort:

op   oke   rimes

Find:

h's and k's

Can you write?:

(Students write words with same patterns)

woke   slop

Can you read?:

(Teacher writes the word for them to read)

crop   broke

Practice:

Practice the common pattern *oke* in "Jack and Jill" and "Little Bo Peep" in Appendix A.

Lesson 34

Letters: e o c h k m r s t

Make:

coke

choke

smoke

smock

mock

rock

sock

shock

stock

stoke

stroke
(CHALLENGE)

Sort:

ock   oke   rimes

Find:

c's and s's

Can you write?:
(Students write words with same patterns)

joke   block

Can you read?:
(Teacher writes the word for them to read)

flock   spoke

Practice:
Practice the common pattern *ock* in "The Cat and the Fiddle," "The Ten O'Clock Scholar," and "Hickory Dickory Dock" in Appendix A.

Letters: e o b c h k r s t

Make:

ore

core

score

store

stoke

choke

chore

shore

sore

bore

broke

coke

stroke

(CHALLENGE)

Sort:

ore   oke   rimes

Find:

t's and k's

Can you write?:

(Students write words with same patterns)

poke   tore

Can you read?:

(Teacher writes the word for them to read)

snore   smoke

Practice:

Practice the common pattern *oke* in "Jack and Jill" and "Little Bo Peep" in Appendix A.

Letters: e i c d n p r t w

Make:

ice

twice

dice

rice

price

pride

ride

tide

wide

side

prices
(CHALLENGE)

Sort:

ide   ice   rimes

Find:

c's and e's

Can you write?:

(Students write words with same patterns)

hide   spice

Can you read?:

(Teacher writes the word for them to read)

slice   glide

Practice:

Practice the common pattern *ice* in "Ding, Dong Bell" and "Birds of a Feather" in Appendix A.

Letters: e i d n p r t w

Make:

in

din

win

wine

wide

ride

tide

tin

pin

pine

dine

pride
(CHALLENGE)

twine
(CHALLENGE)

Sort:

in   ine   ide   rimes

Find:

w's and n's

Can you write?:

(Students write words with same patterns)

nine   slide

Can you read?:

(Teacher writes the word for them to read)

bride   shine

Practice:

Practice the common pattern *ide* in "Old Mother Hubbard" and "Banbury Cross" in Appendix A.

Letters: e i d f l l m n p

Make:

in

fin

fine

pine

pin

line

dine

dill

pill

fill

mill

mine

pile

(CHALLENGE)

Sort:

in   ine   ill   rimes

Find:

d's and p's

Can you write?:

(Students write words with same patterns)

shin   twine

Can you read?:

(Teacher writes the word for them to read)

spine   spill

Practice:

Practice the common pattern *ine* in "1, 2 Buckle My Shoe," "Birds of a Feather," and "Pease Porridge" in Appendix A.

Letters: e i c f k l m n p

Make:

in

kin

fin

fine

pine

line

mine

mice

nice

lice

lick

pick

nick

kiln

(CHALLENGE)

Sort:

ice   ine   ick   rimes

Find:

l's and k's

Can you write?:

(Students write words with same patterns)

stick   shine

Can you read?:

(Teacher writes the word for them to read)

dice   thick

Practice:

Practice the common patterns *ine* and *ice* in "Birds of a Feather" in Appendix A.

Lesson 40

Letters: a c l p s t w

Make:

at

cat

pat/

tap

lap

law

paw

saw

caw

cap

sap

sat

claw

(CHALLENGE)

Sort:

at   ap   aw   rimes

Find:

t's and l's

Can you write?:

(Students write words with same patterns)

jaw   snap

Can you read?:

(Teacher writes the word for them to read)

trap   raw

Practice:

Practice the common pattern *at* in "Jack Sprat," "Thirty Days Hath September," and "Little Miss Muffet" in Appendix A.

Lesson 41
Letters: a l p r s t w y

Make:

way

lay

law

saw

say

pay

paw

raw

ray

pray

stay

straw
(CHALLENGE)

stray
(CHALLENGE)

Sort:

aw   ay   rimes

Find:

w's and y's

Can you write?:

(Students write words with same patterns)

hay   draw

Can you read?:

(Teacher writes the word for them to read)

slaw   Monday

Practice:

Practice the common patterns *aw* and *ay* in "The Hobby Horse" and "Billy Billy," or *ay* in "Rain" and "Cock-Crow" in Appendix A.

Easy Lessons for Teaching Word Families • Scholastic Professional Books

Lesson 42
Letters: a l m p r s w

Review the two sounds of *a* used in this lesson.

Make:

ma

pa

paw

pan

ran

raw

saw

sap

map

man

ran

rap

lap

law

slaw

(CHALLENGE)

Sort:

an   ap   aw   rimes

Find:

m's and w's

Can you write?:

(Students write words with same patterns)

draw   nap

Can you read?:

(Teacher writes the word for them to read)

thaw   snap

Practice:

Practice the common pattern *an* in "Georgy Porgy," "I Saw a Ship A-Sailing," and "Banbury Cross" in Appendix A.

Letters: a y h m n p r s s

Make:

an

man

pan

ran

rash

sash

say

pay

ray

may

mash

smash
(CHALLENGE)

pray
(CHALLENGE)

Sort:

an   ay   ash   rimes

Find:

y's and h's

Can you write?:

(Students write words with same patterns)

smash   clay

Can you read?:

(Teacher writes the word for them to read)

spray   hash

Practice:

Practice the common pattern *ash* in "If All the Seas" or *ay* in "Rain" in Appendix A.

Easy Lessons for Teaching Word Families • Scholastic Professional Books

Letters: o g h l n p r s t

Make:

so
go
no
not
pot
lot
got
rot
hot
hop
lop
top
stop
gosh
(CHALLENGE)
ghost
(CHALLENGE)

Sort:

ot   op   o   rimes

Find:

h's and n's

Can you write?:

(Students write words with same patterns)

shot   flop

Can you read?:

(Teacher writes the word for them to read)

shop   trot

Practice:

Practice the common pattern *ot* in "Simple Simon," "Old Mother Hubbard," and "Pease Porridge" in Appendix A.

Lesson 45

Letters: i b f g h l r s t

Make:

it

lit

light

right

sight

sit

slit

bit

fit

flit

fight

slight
(CHALLENGE)

Sort:

it   ight   rimes

Find:

r's and h's

Can you write?:

(Students write words with same patterns)

split   night

Can you read?:

(Teacher writes the word for them to read)

fright   skit

Practice:

Practice the common pattern *it* in "The Hobby Horse," "The Greedy Man," "Rain," and "If All the Seas" in Appendix A.

Lesson 46
Letters: i g h k l n r s t

Make:

king

sting

sing

sink

sight

night

right

ring

rink

link

light

slight
(CHALLENGE)

Sort:

ink   ing   ight   rimes

Find:

l's and h's

Can you write?:

(Students write words with same patterns)

stink   sting

Can you read?:

(Teacher writes the word for them to read)

fling   bright

Practice:

Practice the common pattern *ing* in "Thirty Days Hath September," "Humpty Dumpty," and "Ding Dong Bell" in Appendix A.

Letters: i b f g h n r s t

Make:

in
fin
tin
bin
bit
hit
sit
fit
fight
sight
night
right
fright
(CHALLENGE)
bright
(CHALLENGE)

Sort:

in   it   ight   rimes

Find:

r's and n's

Can you write?:

(Students write words with same patterns)

tight   skin

Can you read?:

(Teacher writes the word for them to read)

slit   slight

Practice:

Practice the common patterns *it* and *ight* in "Little Miss Muffet" in Appendix A.

Easy Lessons for Teaching Word Families • Scholastic Professional Books

Lesson 48

Letters: a u b c d k l n p r

Make:

an
ban
ran
pan
plan
plank
blank
clank
crank
drank
drunk
dunk
bunk
punk
plunk
(CHALLENGE)

Sort:

an   ank   unk   rimes

Find:

u's and n's

Can you write?:

(Students write words with same patterns)

lank   chunk

Can you read?:

(Teacher writes the word for them to read)

trunk   shrank

Practice:

Practice the common pattern *an* in "Ladybird," "Georgy Porgy," and "Pat-a-Cake" in Appendix A.

Scholastic Professional Books • *Easy Lessons for Teaching Word Families*

Letters: a i l n p r s t

Make:

in
tin
pin
pain
rain
rip
rap
tip
nip
nap
nail
rail
sail
snail
sprain
(CHALLENGE)
trail
(CHALLENGE)

Sort:

ail ain in ip rimes

Find:

l's and t's

Can you write?:

(Students write words with same patterns)

jail   gain

Can you read?:

(Teacher writes the word for them to read)

brain   mail

Practice:

Practice the common pattern *ain*
in "Rain" in Appendix A.

Letters: a e o c f g l m r

Make:

ore

core

care

fare

fore

fame

game

gore

more

lore

lame

flame

glare

(CHALLENGE)

Sort:

ame   ore   are   rimes

Find:

m's and r's

Can you write?:

(Students write words with same patterns)

name   store

Can you read?:

(Teacher writes the word for them to read)

shore   blame

Practice:

Practice the common pattern *ame* in "Georgy Porgy" and "Old Mother Hubbard" in Appendix A.

Lesson 51
Letters: a i l n p r s t

Make:

tan
pan
pal
pail
pain
rain
rail
sail
tail
nail
nap
lap
rap
rip
lip
snail
(CHALLENGE)
train
(CHALLENGE)

Sort:

ail ain ip ap rimes

Find:

i's and l's

Can you write?:

(Students write words with same patterns)

trail   scrap

Can you read?:

(Teacher writes the word for them to read)

strap   mail

Practice:

Practice the common pattern *ail* in "The Hobby Horse," "Simple Simon," and "Little Bo Peep" in Appendix A.

Easy Lessons for Teaching Word Families • Scholastic Professional Books

Letters: a i l l m p s t

Make:

sap

sip

lip

tip

tap

lap/

pal

pail

pill

sill

sail

tail

mail

mill

still
(CHALLENGE)

lips
(CHALLENGE)

Sort:

ail   ill   ip   ap   rimes

Find:

t's and i's

Can you write?:

(Students write words with same patterns)

snap   snail

Can you read?:

(Teacher writes the word for them to read)

kill   flip

Practice:

Practice the common pattern *ill* in "Birds of a Feather," "Little Bo Peep," and "Little Boy Blue" in Appendix A.

Letters: a e h l m n p s t

Make:

ate

mate/

meat

heat/

hate

Nate/ *Note that you need a capital.*

neat

peat

pleat/

plate

late

slate

(CHALLENGE)

plates

(CHALLENGE)

Sort:

ate   eat   rimes

Find:

p's and a's

Can you write?:

(Students write words with same patterns)

gate   heat

Can you read?:

(Teacher writes the word for them to read)

treat   state

Practice:

Practice the common pattern *eat* in "The Pumpkin Eater," "Little Miss Muffet," and "Sing a Song" in Appendix A.

Letters: a e u g h l m r t

Make:

tag
tug/
gut
get
gate
rate
rag
rug
lug
lag
late
mate
mug
hug
hate
grate
(CHALLENGE)

Sort:

ate   ug   rimes

Find:

r's and u's

Can you write?:

(Students write words with same patterns)

state   slug

Can you read?:

(Teacher writes the word for them to read)

chug   slate

Practice:

Practice the common pattern *ate* in "The Greedy Man" and "Cock-Crow" in Appendix A.

Letters: a i b k n p r s t

Make:

pin
pain
pan
plan
plank
bank
ban
bran
brain
stain
stank
sank
sink
rink
rank
rain
strain
(CHALLENGE)
brink
(CHALLENGE)

Sort:

ain an ank in ink rimes

Find:

p's and b's

Can you write?:

(Students write words with same patterns)

thank   think

Can you read?:

(Teacher writes the word for them to read)

blink   train

Practice:

Practice the common pattern *ink* in "Twinkle Twinkle Little Star" and "Cross Patch" in Appendix A.

Easy Lessons for Teaching Word Families • Scholastic Professional Books

Appendix A

Included in Appendix A are some of your favorite nursery rhymes to use for reading practice and as an opportunity to work with common word patterns/chunks. Over a period of one to two weeks, work on phonics with the poem in a pocket chart on sentence strips.

WHOLE GROUP WORK

1. Read the poem to students and then with them.

2. Read the poem in a variety of ways.

3. "Who can find _____?"
   - sentences, words, letters
   - chunks/word patterns from Words Lessons

4. Group work:
   - Mix up sentence strips and rebuild the poem.
   - Match with extra sentence strips, then words and letters.
   - Substitutions: "I'm going to trick you, look closely."
      Inventions: Substitute word cards that change the poem.
      Errors: Substitute letters that will change the poem.
      Spoonerisms: Switch letters from words that are in the poem.

SMALL GROUP WORK

1. Make two copies of the poem for each student.
2. Read the poem from the personal copy.
3. Cut the second copy of the poem into sentence strips.
   - Match on top of the personal copy.
   - Rebuild on the table without matching.
4. Cut the second copy of the poem into individual words.
   - Match on top of the second copy.
   - Rebuild on the table without matching.
5. Take home in an envelope one copy of the poem and the poem cut into separate words.

INDEPENDENT WORK IN A POETRY CENTER

Run five copies of the poem on colored cardstock.
   - two copies mounted on 9-by-12-inch manila envelopes for storage
   - one copy cut into a poem puzzle (store in one large envelope)
   - one copy cut into sentence strips for matching and rebuilding
   - one copy cut into words for matching and rebuilding
   (store sentences and words in second large envelope)

NURSERY RHYMES	RIMES	LESSON NUMBERS
1,2 Buckle My Shoe	at, ay, ick, ight, ine, uck	2, 13, 38
Banbury Cross	an, ell, ide, ing, ock	10, 16, 37, 42
Billy, Billy	aw, ay, ight, ill, ine, ing, ip	19, 41, 52
Birds of a Feather	at, ice, ill, ine, ock	5, 36, 38, 39, 52
Cock-Crow	ate, ay, ell, ill, ock	16, 30, 41, 54
Cross Patch	ake, aw, in, ink, it	7, 11, 55
Ding, Dong Bell	at, ell, ice, ill, in, ing, it	12, 20, 36, 46
Georgy Porgy	ame, an, ay, ing	1, 42, 48, 50
Hickory, Dickory Dock	an, ick, ock, uck	5, 13, 27, 34
Humpty Dumpty	at, ing, ot, ump	12, 14, 15, 46
I Saw a Ship A-Sailing	ack, ail, ain, an, ap, aw, ice, in, ing, ip, it, uck	8, 19, 42
If All the Seas Were One Sea	an, ash, at, eat, in, it	23, 43, 45
Jack and Jill	ack, ail, ame, ell, ill, ing, oke	7, 10, 16, 17, 29, 33, 35
Jack Sprat	ack, at, eat, ick	3, 21, 40, 48
Little Bo Peep	ail, eat, ell, ill, ing, it, oke	17, 33, 35, 51, 52, 53
Little Boy Blue	ack, ake, ay, ill, in, it, ot	4, 26, 28, 52
Little Miss Muffet	ame, at, ay, eat, ight, ing, it	3, 20, 40, 47, 53
Old Mother Hubbard	ack, all, ame, at, ide, ing, ot	10, 24, 37, 44, 50
Pat-a-Cake	ake, an, at, ick, in, it	2, 7, 23, 48
Pease Porridge	ay, in, ine, it, ot	4, 24, 38, 44
Rain	ain, an, ay, it	41, 43, 45, 49
Rock-a-Bye Baby	ill, ock, op	6, 25, 27
Simple Simon	ail, ale, an, ay, ick, ing, ot	1, 24, 28, 44, 51
Sing a Song	ack, ake, ame, an, ap, at, eat, in, ing, ock, ot	4, 5, 6, 9, 27, 28, 31, 53
The Cat and the Fiddle	an, at, ay, it, ump	1, 15, 20, 23, 34
The Clever Hen	ake, ale, an, at, ill, it	7, 26, 28, 32
The Greedy Man	ake, an, ate, it	30, 45, 54
The Hobby Horse	ail, an, ap, aw, ay, ing, it	12, 31, 41, 45, 51
The Pumpkin Eater	eat, ell, in, ump	14, 16, 17, 53
The Ten O'Clock Scholar	ake, at, ill, ock	2, 6, 26, 34
Thirty Days Hath September	at, ay, est, ing	3, 18, 40, 46
Twinkle Twinkle Little Star	in, ink it	11, 12, 55

Easy Lessons for Teaching Word Families • Scholastic Professional Books

1, 2, Buckle My Shoe

1, 2,   Buckle my shoe

3, 4,   Shut the door

5, 6,   Pick up sticks

7, 8,   Lay them straight

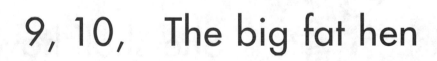

9, 10,   The big fat hen

Banbury Cross

Ride a cock-horse

To Banbury Cross,

To see an old lady

Upon a white horse.

Rings on her fingers

And bells on her toes,

She shall have music

Wherever she goes.

Easy Lessons for Teaching Word Families • Scholastic Professional Books

Billy, Billy

"Billy, Billy come and play,
While the sun shines bright as day

"Yes, my Polly, so I will,
For I love to please you still."

"Billy, Billy, have you seen
Sam and Betsy on the green?"

"Yes, my Poll, I saw them pass,
Skipping o'er the new-mown grass."

"Billy, Billy, come along,
And I will sing a pretty song."

Birds of a Feather

Birds of a feather flock together

And so do pigs and swine:

Rats and mice will have their choice,

And so will I have mine.

Easy Lessons for Teaching Word Families • Scholastic Professional Books

Cock-Crow

Cocks crow in the morn
To tell us to rise,

And he who lies late
Will never be wise;

For early to bed
And early to rise,

Is the way to be healthy
And wealthy and wise.

Cross Patch

Cross patch, draw the latch,

Sit by the fire and spin;

Take a cup and drink it up,

Then call your neighbors in.

Easy Lessons for Teaching Word Families • Scholastic Professional Books

Ding, Dong, Bell

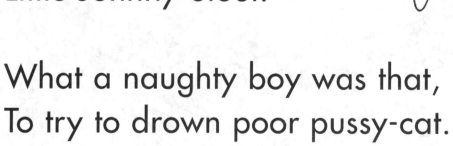

Ding, dong, bell,
Pussy's in the well!

Who put her in?
Little Tommy Lin.

Who pulled her out?
Little Johnny Stout.

What a naughty boy was that,
To try to drown poor pussy-cat.

Who never did him any harm,
But killed the mice in his
father's barn!

Georgy Porgy

Georgy Porgy, pudding and pie,

Kissed the girls and made them cry,

When the boys came out to play,

Georgy Porgy ran away.

Easy Lessons for Teaching Word Families • Scholastic Professional Books

Hickory, Dickory, Dock

Hickory, dickory, dock,

The mouse ran up the

clock.

The clock struck one,

The mouse ran down,

Hickory, dickory, dock.

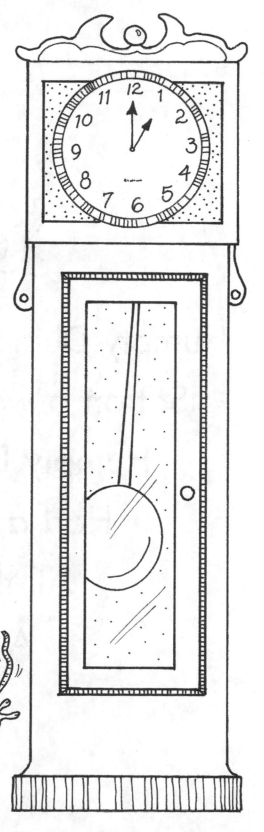

Humpty Dumpty

Humpty Dumpty
Sat on a wall.
Humpty Dumpty
Had a great fall.
All the king's horses
And all the king's men
Cannot put Humpty
Dumpty together again.

Easy Lessons for Teaching Word Families • Scholastic Professional Books

If All the Seas Were One Sea

If all the seas were one sea,
What a great sea that would be!

And if all the trees were one tree,
What a great tree that would be!

And if all the axes were one ax,
What a great ax that would be!

And if all the men were one man,
What a great man he would be!

And if the great man took the great ax
And cut down the great tree,

And let it fall into the great sea,
What a splish splash that would be!

I Saw a Ship A-Sailing

I saw a ship a sailing
A-sailing on the sea;
And, oh! it was all laden
With pretty things for thee!

There were comfits in the cabin,
And apples in the hold;
The sails were made of silk,
And the masts were made of gold.

The four-and-twenty sailors
That stood between the decks,
Were four-and-twenty white mice
With chains about their necks.

The captain was a duck,
With a packet on his back;
And when the ship began to move,
The captain said, "Quack! Quack!"

Easy Lessons for Teaching Word Families • Scholastic Professional Books

Jack and Jill

Jack and Jill

    Went up the hill,

        To fetch a pail of water;

        Jack fell down

        And broke his crown,

        And Jill

          came

            tumbling

              after.

Jack Sprat

Jack Sprat could eat no fat,

His wife could eat no lean.

So between them both you see,

They licked the platter clean.

Easy Lessons for Teaching Word Families • Scholastic Professional Books

Little Bo-Peep

Little Bo-Peep has lost her sheep,
And can't tell where to find them;

Leave them alone,
And they'll come home,
And bring their tails behind them.

Little Bo-Peep fell fast asleep,
And dreamt she heard them bleating;

But when she awoke,
She found it a joke,
For still they all were fleeting.

Little Boy Blue

Little Boy Blue,
    Come blow your horn,
The sheep's in the meadow,
    The cow's in the corn.
Where is the boy
    Who looks after the sheep?
He's under the haycock
    Fast asleep.
Will you wake him?
    No, not I,
For if I do,
    He's sure to cry.

Easy Lessons for Teaching Word Families • Scholastic Professional Books

Little Miss Muffet

Little Miss Muffet
    Sat on a tuffet,
      Eating her curds and
      whey;
There came a big spider,
    Who sat down beside her
    And frightened Miss
    Muffet away.

Old Mother Hubbard

Old Mother Hubbard went to the cupboard
To give her poor dog a bone;

But when she got there, the cupboard was bare,
And so the poor dog had none.

She went to the hatter's to buy him a hat;
when she came back he was feeding the cat.

She went to the barber's to buy him a wig;
When she came back he was dancing a jig.

She went to the tailor's to buy him a coat;
When she came back, he was riding a goat.

She went to the cobbler's to buy him some shoes;
When she came back he was reading the news.

Easy Lessons for Teaching Word Families • Scholastic Professional Books

Pat-a-Cake

Pat-a-cake, pat-a-cake,

Baker's man!

Bake me a cake

As fast as you can.

Pat it, and prick it,

And mark it with T,

Put it in the oven

For Tommy and me.

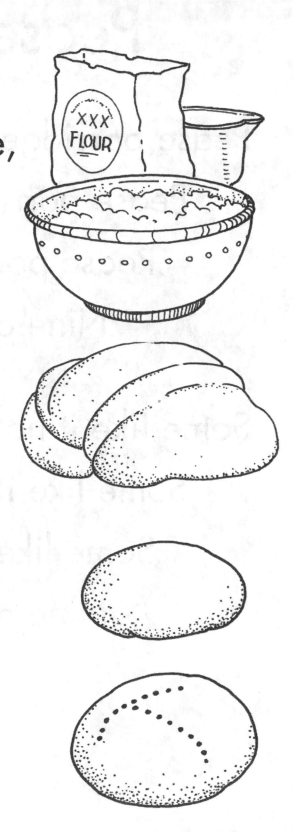

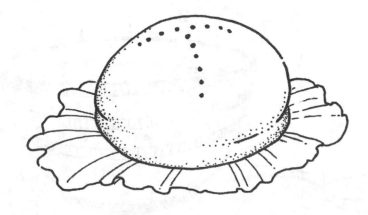

Pease Porridge

Pease porridge hot,
Pease porridge cold,
Pease porridge in the pot,
Nine days old.

Some like it hot,
Some like it cold,
Some like it in the pot,
Nine days old.

Easy Lessons for Teaching Word Families • Scholastic Professional Books

Rain

Rain, rain, go away,

Come again

another day;

Little Johnny wants

to play.

Rock-a-bye Baby

Rock-a-bye baby
On the treetop,
When the wind blows
The cradle will rock;
When the bough breaks
The cradle will fall,
And down will come
        baby,
Cradle, and all.

Easy Lessons for Teaching Word Families • Scholastic Professional Books

Simple Simon

Simple Simon met a pieman,
Going to the fair:
Says Simple Simon to the pieman,
"Let me taste your ware."

Says the pieman to Simple Simon,
"Show me first your penny."
Says Simple Simon to the pieman,
"Indeed I have not any."

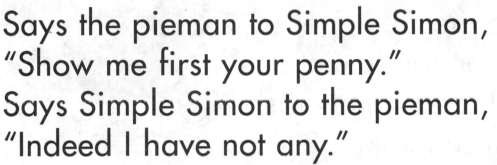

Simple Simon went a fishing,
For to catch a whale;
All the water he had got
Was in his mother's pail.

Simple Simon went to look
If plums grew on a thistle;
He pricked his fingers very much,
Which made poor Simon whistle.

Sing a Song

Sing a song of sixpence,
A pocket full of rye.
Four-and-twenty blackbirds
Baked in a pie.

When the pie was opened,
The birds began to sing.
Was not that a dainty dish
To set before the king?

The king was in the counting-house,
Counting out his money.
The queen was in the parlor,
Eating bread and honey.

The maid was in the garden,
Hanging out the clothes.
When down came a blackbird
And snapped off her nose!

Easy Lessons for Teaching Word Families • Scholastic Professional Books

The Cat and the Fiddle

Hey diddle, diddle!
The cat and the fiddle,
The cow jumped over
   the moon.
The little dog laughed
To see such a sport
And the dish ran away
   with the spoon.

The Clever Hen

I had a little hen,
the prettiest ever seen,

She washed me the dishes
and kept the house clean.

She went to the mill
to fetch me some flour

She brought it home
in less than an hour;

She baked me my bread,
she brewed me my ale,

She sat by the fire
and told many a fine tale.

Easy Lessons for Teaching Word Families • Scholastic Professional Books

The Greedy Man

The greedy man is he who sits

And bites bits out of plates,

Or else takes up an almanac

And gobbles all the dates.

Scholastic Professional Books • Easy Lessons for Teaching Word Families

The Hobby Horse

I had a little hobby-horse,
And it was dapple gray;

Its head was made of pea-straw,
Its tail was made of hay.

I sold it to an old woman
For a copper groat;

And I'll not sing my song again
Without another coat.

Easy Lessons for Teaching Word Families • Scholastic Professional Books

The Pumpkin Eater

Peter, Peter, pumpkin eater,

Had a wife and couldn't keep her;

He put her in a pumpkin shell,

And there he kept her very well.

The Ten O'Clock Scholar

A diller, a dollar,
A ten o'clock scholar

What makes you
Come so soon?

You used to come
At ten o'clock,

But now you come
At noon.

Easy Lessons for Teaching Word Families • Scholastic Professional Books

Thirty Days Hath September

Thirty days hath September,

April, June, and November;

February has twenty-eight alone,

All the rest have thirty-one,

Excepting leap-year, that's the time

When February's days are twenty-nine.

Twinkle, Twinkle Little Star

Twinkle, Twinkle,
little star,

How I wonder
what you are!

Up above the world
so high,

Like a diamond
in the sky.

Twinkle, Twinkle,
little star,

How I wonder
what you are!

Easy Lessons for Teaching Word Families • Scholastic Professional Books

Appendix B

Large letter cards are used to manipulate letters in the pocket chart for the small group to check. The black line masters are ready to be run on heavy paper such as cardstock. Run the vowels on pink cardstock and the consonants on white. With the vowels in a different color, the vowel patterns are easily visible.

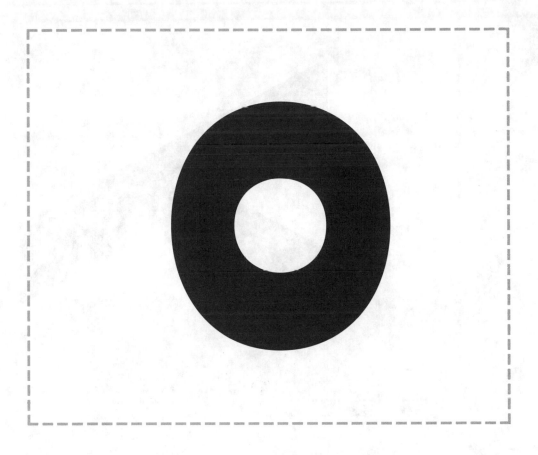

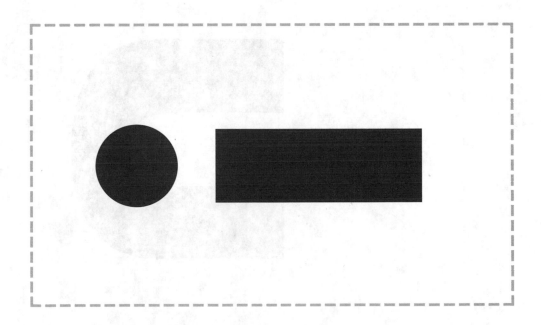

Scholastic Professional Books • Easy Lessons for Teaching Word Families

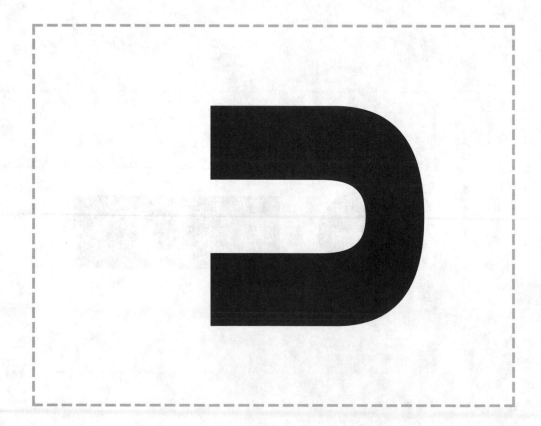

Easy Lessons for Teaching Word Families • Scholastic Professional Books

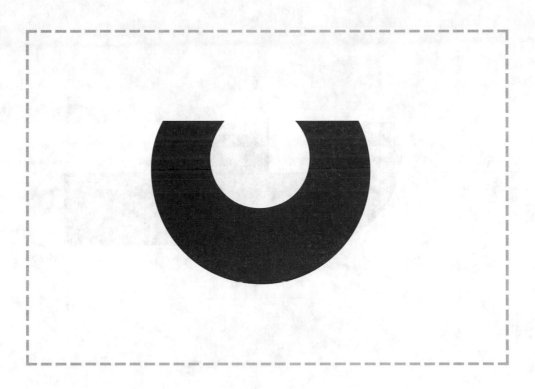

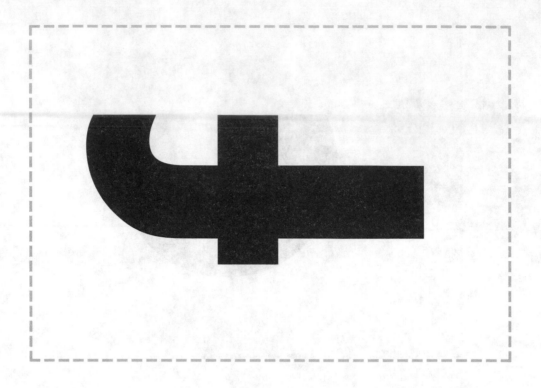

Easy Lessons for Teaching Word Families • Scholastic Professional Books

Easy Lessons for Teaching Word Families • Scholastic Professional Books

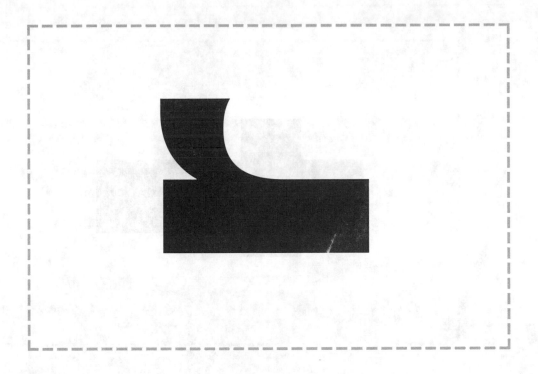

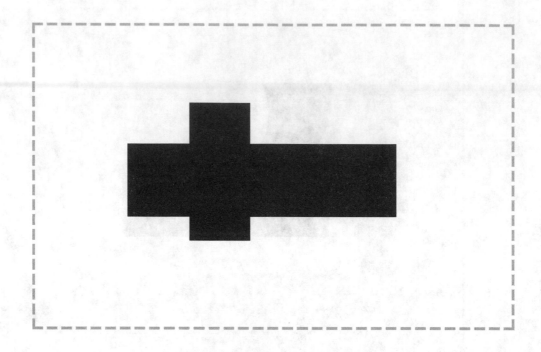

Easy Lessons for Teaching Word Families • Scholastic Professional Books

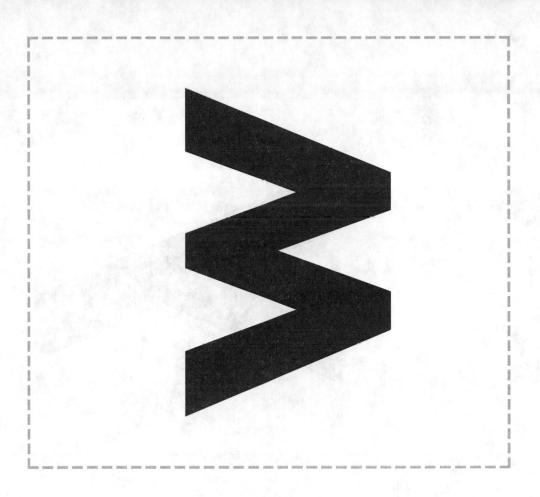

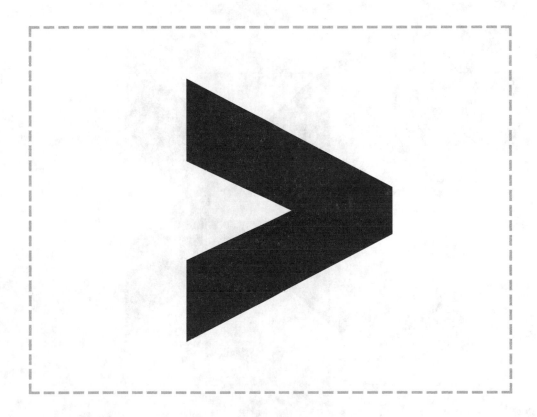

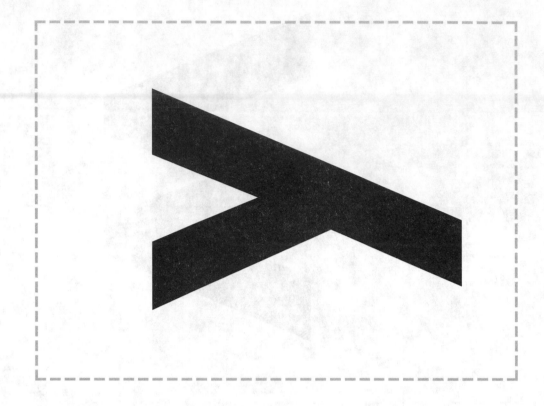

Appendix C

Print small letters for students to manipulate as they make words. Print vowels on pink card-stock and the consonnants on white cardstock so that vowel patterns are visible.

How many should I print for my classroom?

For small group work, 40 of each letter will last for many years. Vowels are seven to a page, so copy six of each vowel page on pink. Consonants are two to a page, so copy twenty of each consonant page on white. Extra letters can be run for an ABC Center.

How should I store my letters?

• small sandwich bags kept in a basket or tub (all of the same letter in one bag)
• plastic drawer case, found with tool kits at places like Target, K-Mart, Walmart, Sears, etc. The ideal has 30 drawers. Each drawer is passed for students to take out letters needed for a particular lesson.

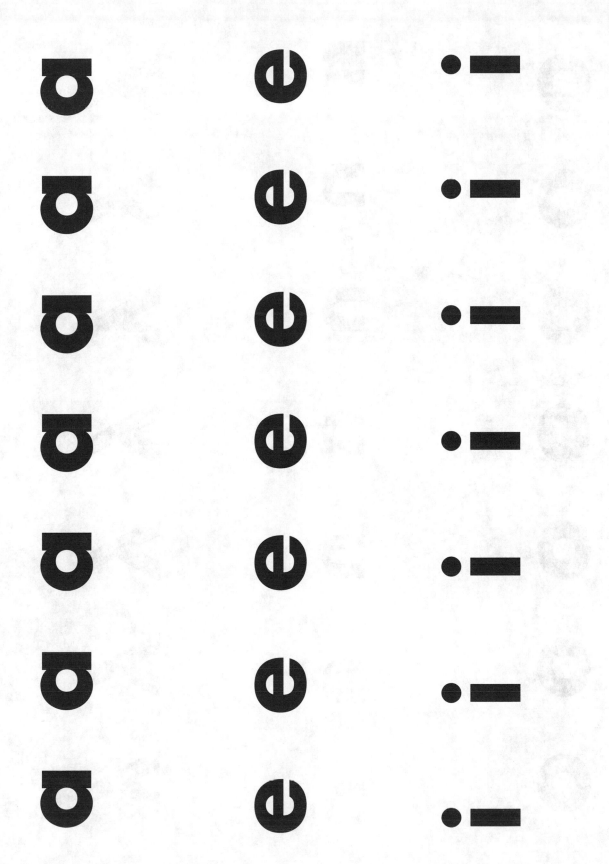

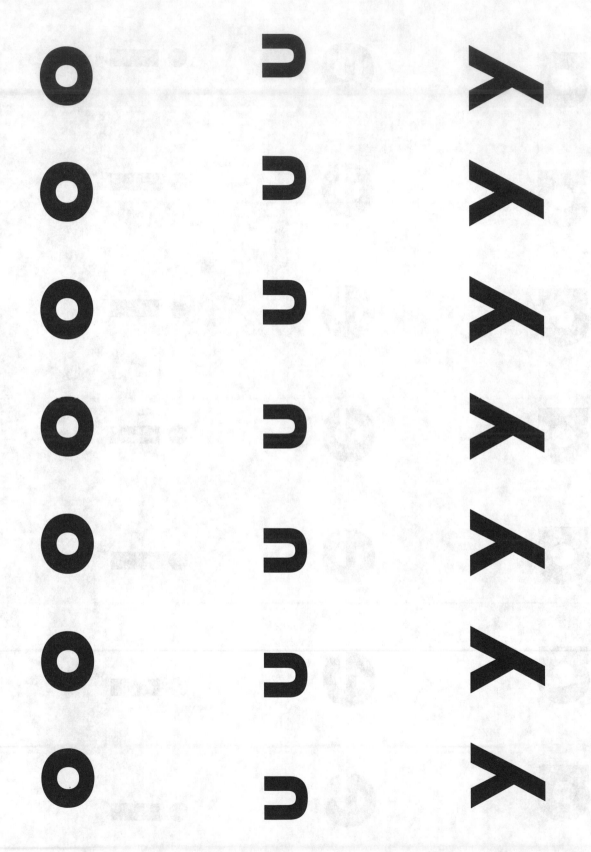

f d f

b c d

b c

j h j

f g h

k l m n

k l m u

Scholastic Professional Books • Easy Lessons for Teaching Word Families

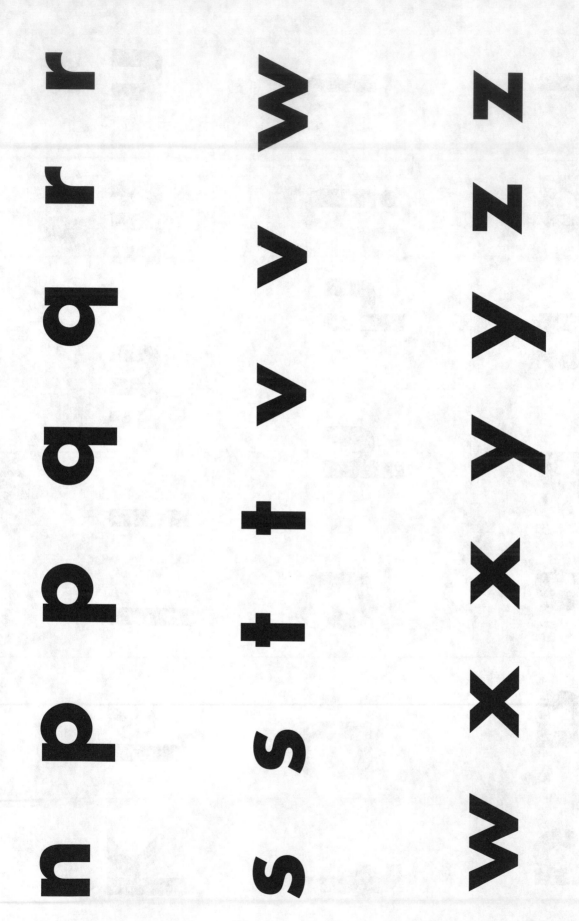

r r

q q

p p

n

w w

v v

t t

s s

z z

y y

x x

w

Appendix D

Wordboards with letter boxes provide a workspace while children build words. Run the workspaces on cardstock.

Choose the wordboard that matches the majority of words in the lesson you are doing. For example, if the majority of the words are 3 letter words, use the wordboard with 3 boxes. If there is an occasional word with an extra letter, teach students to put it after the last box.

Teach students to "push sounds in boxes." This technique from Reading Recovery® forces students to say a word slowly and match each sound with a box going left to right. Model and practice:

1. Put their finger under the first box and say the first sound only as they move their finger up into the box.

2. Hold that sound as they move their finger down under the next box. Say the next sound as their finger moves into the corresponding box.

3. Continue for each box and sound that matches.

4. Coach: What do you hear? Where do you hear it?

5. Students match letters to the sound they heard and make changes in boxes where a new word necessitates a change.

6. Whenever a student has trouble, repeat this method.

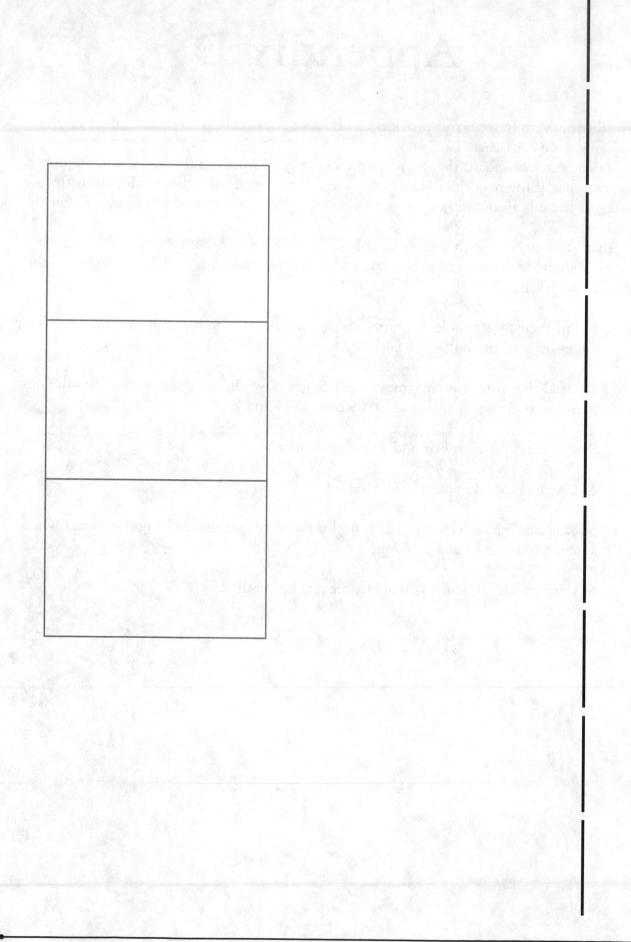

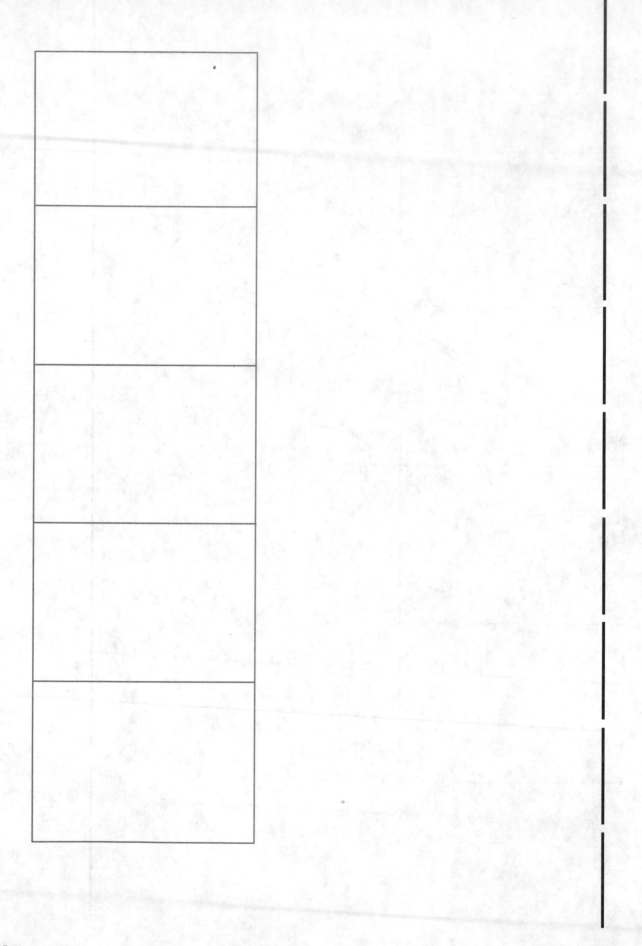

Professional Resources

Adams, Marilyn, *Beginning to Read: Thinking and Learning Print About Print.* Cambridge: M.I.T Press, 1990.

Bear, Donald R., Shane Templeton, Marcia Invernizzi, & Francine Johnston, *Words Their Way: Word Study for Phonics, Vocabulary, and Spelling Instruction,* Merrill/Prentice-Hall, 1996.

Cunningham, Patricia., Dorothy Hall, *Making Words,* Carthage, Illinois: Good Apple, 1994.

Cunningham, Patricia., Dorothy Hall, *Making Big Words,* Parsippany, New Jersey: Good Apple, 1994.

Cunningham, Patricia., *Phonics They Use,* New York: Harper Collins, 1995.

Cunningham, Patricia., Dorothy Hall, *Making More Words,* Parsippany, New Jersey: Good Apple, 1997.

Goswami, U., and Bryant, P., *Phonological Skills and Learning to Read.* East Sussex, UK: Erlbaum Associated, 1990.

Johnson, Terry and Daphne Louis, *Literacy Through Literature,* Portsmouth, NH: Heinemann, 1987.

Trieman, R. "Onsets and Rimes as Units of Spoken Syllables: Evidence from Children," *Journal of Experimental Child Psychology,* 39, 161–181, 1985.

Wagstaff, Janiel. *Phonics That Work,* New York: Scholastic, 1994.

Young, Sue, *The Scholastic Rhyming Dictionary,* New York: Scholastic, 1994.

Videos are available for staff development on *Making Words* and *Easy Lessons for Teaching Word Families.* Judy models these strategies with kindergartners, and first and second graders from her school. Contact: Bureau of Education and Research
P.O. Box 96068
Bellevue, WA 98009
(800) 735-3503

Judy Lynch is a full-time teacher at Madison Elementary School near Sacramento, California. She is a Reading Recovery® teacher and teaches with an incredible K–3 team doing literacy support. When she is not teaching, Judy works with teachers and school districts across the United States and Canada. Her passion is teaching *all* children to read. Her journey in early literacy includes a reading specialist credential and a masters in reading and language arts. All of her study of research and new strategies has been applied to the first graders and other primary students she teaches. Judy has been married for 28 years to a football coach and they have three great children and a rambunctious Irish setter.

Easy Lessons for Teaching Word Families • Scholastic Professional Books

The Random House Book of
OPERA STORIES

Retold by Adèle Geras

Illustrations by
Ian Beck
Louise Brierley
Emma Chichester Clark
Susan Field
Katya Mikhailovsky
Sheila Moxley
Jane Ray
Sophie Windham

Costume designs by Rosemary Vercoe

Random House 🏠 New York

CONTENTS

Wolfgang Amadeus Mozart
1756-91

By the time he was six, Mozart was giving concerts in
royal palaces all over Europe. He is one of the very
greatest of composers, and his music is loved
throughout the world.

Mozart wrote The Magic Flute (Die Zauberflöte)
in 1791, the year of his early death. He devised it with his
friend Emanuel Schikaneder who took the role of Papageno
(which perhaps explains why Papageno has so much to do!).
Schikaneder was the director of a theatre company and very
fond of magic and special effects. The opera is full of them.
Mozart's own sister-in-law was the first Queen of the Night
and Mozart himself once played Papageno's bells during a
performance.

Though the story itself is rather eccentric, in the opera
house The Magic Flute is a most moving theatrical
experience. A famous critic described it as the only opera in
existence "that might conceivably have been composed
by God".

THE MAGIC FLUTE

The Test of True Love

The story I'm going to tell you is about so many strange and wonderful things that I fear you may become dizzy with the wonders of it. You will see dragons and angels, and visit temples and dungeons; old crones will change into beautiful young women, a young couple will walk through fire. You'll tremble before the Queen of the Night, and hear the melody of the magic flute, whose music weaves through the story like a silver thread. But for all its complications, this is a tale about two very different couples and how they each find True Love.

Let us begin with the Queen of the Night. She ruled the dark sky and wore the stars as jewels on her gown. No one dared to disobey her, for she was very powerful. She had three ladies who carried out her orders, and one day they looked down to earth and saw a prince running and running to escape the clutches of a ferocious, scaly dragon.

"Quick!" said the first lady. "We must save him! He is Prince Tamino." And the three ladies took their weapons and pierced the creature through the heart.

The dragon sank to the ground, stuck all over with silver spears, and the Prince stumbled and fell and lay quite still. The three ladies looked down at him.

"Oh, he's very handsome, isn't he?" said the first. "But the poor young man is stunned. We must tell the Queen about this at once."

"You two go," said the second lady, stroking Tamino's brow, "and I'll stay here and see that he comes to no harm."

"No, sister," said the third lady. "We will all go together."

And they vanished in an instant.

Suddenly the air was filled with the trilling, happy music of the pipes, and along came Papageno. He was bird-catcher to the Queen of the Night, and was hung about with cages. He was singing his favourite song: the one about what a fine bird-catcher he was.

"Oh, my fluttered feathers! What's been going on here?" he said, nearly tripping over Tamino's body. "Someone has had an accident, I see."

He put his cages down, and it was only then that he caught sight of the dragon's body. This gave him such a fright that he almost fainted.

feathered headdress

tattered frockcoat, covered with feathers

patched brocade waistcoat

striped patched trousers

PAPAGENO

"A dragon! Save me! Help me!" he cried. But then he noticed the silver spears. "Ooh, thank goodness for that," he sighed. "The creature's dead as a doornail. Panic over!"

Prince Tamino opened his eyes. First he saw the dead dragon, and then he saw Papageno, who said:

"No need to worry, dear sir. The dragon is dead, and I should know … I killed it myself. No need to thank me. It was nothing, really. Anyone would have done the same."

The three ladies appeared suddenly out of the blue air.

"You are a liar, Papageno," said the first, "and for this we will punish you."

She clamped Papageno's mouth shut with a metal padlock, so that he couldn't make a sound.

"You'll keep silent," she said, "or the Queen of the Night will hear of it."

Papageno trembled. As I've told you already, everyone was afraid of the Queen of the Night.

The ladies turned to Tamino.

"Prince, our mistress commanded us to save you, and she sends you this portrait of her daughter."

Tamino looked at the picture of a beautiful young woman, and at once his heart was filled with love for her.

"Her name is Pamina," said the second lady. "She's been imprisoned by an evil wizard. The Queen herself will tell you

more. Listen, she's coming."

The sky darkened, thunder rumbled in the distance, and all at once the Queen of the Night appeared, in a cloak made of night skies and starlight. Her grandeur and majesty filled Tamino with awe, but he could see that she was sad.

THE QUEEN OF THE NIGHT

indigo silk cloak

embroidered stars

pink brocade underskirt

pink satin slippers

"Hear me, Prince," she sighed, "and learn of my daughter's fate. A wicked enchanter called Sarastro has stolen her away and locked her up, and I cannot bear to be without her. If you will set her free, and bring her back to me, then you shall marry her."

Tamino said: "I'd do anything to win her. But tell me what I must do."

"My ladies will instruct you," said the Queen, and she rose up and up into the clouds and was gone.

"First of all," said the first lady, "this magic flute will help you whenever you need it."

A shining silver instrument appeared in the air above Tamino's head and glittered as it floated down into his hand.

"And of course Papageno will go with you," said the second lady, "to be your helper."

She removed the lock from the bird-catcher's mouth, and he began to speak immediately.

"Listen, dear ladies," he said, "rescuing princesses from evil wizards isn't my cup of tea at all. Bird-catching is all I'm fit for, honestly."

"The Queen has spoken," said the third lady, "and, besides, we'll give you this set of magic bells. Play them whenever you need help."

Papageno took the pretty silver bells, and played a tune that rippled and sparkled like a sunlit stream.

"Lovely!" he said. "Let's hope they can also keep us safe."

"Now, which is the way to Sarastro's castle?" asked Tamino. No one answered. The three ladies had vanished into the blue air.

In their place stood three young boys, who looked like angels.

"We'll show you the way, Tamino," said one. "We're spirits sent to help you at all times. You should go in that direction." He pointed his finger.

"Aren't you going to help me too?" Papageno asked, and one of the angelic boys answered: "Your way lies over there." And he pointed in the opposite direction.

So it was that Tamino and Papageno were separated, and Papageno found himself in Sarastro's castle.

"I'll try this door," he said to himself, and

suddenly he was in Princess Pamina's bedchamber. But who was the evil-looking creature leaning over the Princess as though to kiss her?

"My name," said this man, "is Monostatos, and Sarastro is my master. Princess Pamina is my prisoner, and I shall lock you in with her while I tell my master that you're here."

He strode out, and a heavy key turned in the lock.

"Don't be alarmed, Pamina," said Papageno as the Princess shrank from him in fear. "I'm not sure how I came to be here, but it's your mother's magical doing, I think. Prince Tamino has been chosen to rescue you. He's a brave and handsome prince and I'm his assistant. Papageno the bird-catcher at your service."

He sang a little tune and smiled at her.

"Oh, thank you, Papageno. That hideous Monostatos thinks that I'll agree to be his wife, but I never will. Never."

"Tamino loves you," said Papageno. "I only wish I could find a pretty young lady as well … Papageno seeks Papagena! I've been looking everywhere."

"I'm sure," said Pamina, "that you *will* find someone to love. You have a beautiful voice and you must have a kind heart because you've come here to rescue me."

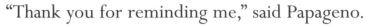

"Thank you for reminding me," said Papageno. "We must get away. If we open the window we'll be able to step out on to the battlements. We mustn't be here when nasty old Monostatos returns."

Pamina and Papageno climbed out of the window and down a flight of steps leading to a courtyard. They had escaped, like two birds flying from a metal cage.

turban and make-up

TIGER

red slippers and gloves

I hope you haven't forgotten about Prince Tamino. He had found his way to the gates of a magnificent temple. He tried to enter, but the gate was locked against him.

"What do you seek?" asked a priest. "This is the temple of Reason and Light."

"I've come to rescue the Princess Pamina from the clutches of the evil wizard Sarastro. Her mother, the Queen of the Night, has charged me with this task."

"You have been tricked," said the priest. "The evil one is the Queen herself, and Sarastro is great and holy. I can explain no more to you now, but you'll understand the truth very soon."

A great darkness then fell over the temple and the lands around it, and a voice spoke out of this darkness, and said: "Princess Pamina is alive. Do not lose courage."

Tamino put the magic flute to his lips and began to play an enchanted tune. Light filled the sky, and every living creature crept out of its hiding-place in rock or tree or sand and approached Tamino, bewitched by his melody. Then the trill of the bird-catcher's pipes came to them on the breeze.

"That's Papageno!" Tamino said. "He must be here somewhere." And he raced off in one direction to look for him, just as Pamina and Papageno appeared from the other direction.

"I heard the magic flute," said Papageno. "So Tamino must have been here."

They didn't see Monostatos creeping up behind them.

"The Prince has gone, but I've hidden here, waiting for you!" he hissed. Then he said to his slaves: "Seize them! Lock them up!"